C000146190

Text: *Neil Coates, Mark Richards, Frank Kew*

Series Editor: *Tony Bowerman*

Photographs: *Neil Coates, Frank Kew, Mark Richards, Steve Thompson, AdobeStock, Alamy, Shutterstock, Dreamstime*

Design: *Carl Rogers and Laura Hodgkinson*

© *Northern Eye Books Limited 2019*

Neil Coates, Mark Richards and Frank Kew have asserted their rights under the Copyright, Designs and Patents Act, 1988 to be identified as the authors of this work. All rights reserved

This book contains mapping data licensed from the Ordnance Survey with the permission of the Controller of Her Majesty's Stationery Office.

© *Crown copyright 2019. All rights reserved. Licence number 100047867*

Northern Eye Books
ISBN 978-1-908632-89-0

A CIP catalogue record for this book is available from the British Library

www.northerneyebooks.co.uk

First published in 2019 by
Northern Eye Books Limited
Northern Eye Books, Tattenhall, Cheshire CH3 9PX
Email: tony@northerneyebooks.com
For sales enquiries, please call 01928 723 744

 @Northerneyeboo

 @northerneyebooks

Cover: Muker meadows, Swaledale (Walk 3)

Contents

The Yorkshire Dales National Park 4

Top 10 Walks: Best of the best 6

1. **The Buck Inn** *Malham* 8

2. **Churchmouse Tea Room** *Barbon* ..14

3. **Muker** *Swaledale* 20

4. **Hardraw Force** *Wensleydale* 26

5. **Pen-y-ghent** *Ribblesdale* 32

6. **Fountains Abbey** *Nidderdale* 36

7. **George & Dragon** *Dent* 42

8. **Uldale Force** *Howgills* 48

9. **Grassington** 52

10. **Ingleborough** 58

Useful Information 64

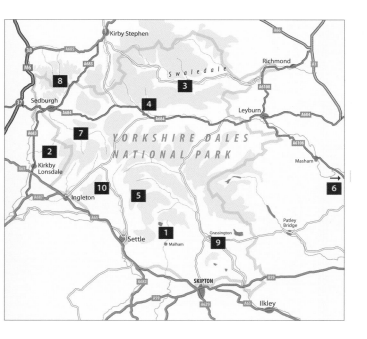

Pennine perfection

Designated in 1954, and extended in 2016, the Yorkshire Dales now cover 2,179 square kilometres/841 square miles of the central Pennines. As well as some of Yorkshire's most magnificent landscapes, the National Park also includes a corner of Cumbria, where the secluded Howgill Fells loom over the River Lune. 'Dales' is something of a misnomer, for in addition to the beautiful dales the area incorporates great tracts of wild moorland, the famous 'Three Peaks' and an intriguing industrial heritage.

Over 1,300 miles of rights of way allow walkers to explore all facets of the Park. In addition, almost 110,000 hectares of open access land has opened up endless possibilities for exploring this heady mix of limestone and gritstone scenery. Upwards of 8 million visitors a year enjoy this striking countryside with its picturesque stone villages.

Stone barns and hay meadows in pretty Swaledale

The very best of the **Yorkshire Dales**

These ten themed walks explore the contrasting faces of
the Yorkshire Dales — the gentle flower-filled Dales and
the wild and rugged uplands with their drystone walls,
waterfalls, limestone pavements and iconic peaks.

Discover unspoiled pubs and friendly teashops. Explore
tiny villages, castles, churches and ancient abbeys. Stroll
beside crystal rivers or thrill to the thunder of some of
Britain's mightiest waterfalls. Conquer the Three Peaks of
Pen-y-ghent, Ingleborough and Whernside. Or just enjoy
the quiet countryside and spectacular scenery. Every walk
here is a walk to savour.

"When God had finished making Heaven, rather like
you make an apple pie, with that bit of pastry that was
left over, he fashioned the Yorkshire Dales."

Russell Harty

TOP 10 **Walks:** The Yorkshire Dales' best walks

HERE, PACKED INTO A SINGLE POCKET-SIZE BOOK, are the ten absolute best short circular walks in the **Yorkshire Dales National Park**. They've been carefully selected — from the already hugely-popular themed *Top 10 Walks: Yorkshire Dales* series — to showcase the finest and most enjoyable walks across Yorkshire. So, whether you fancy an easy stroll in a flower-decked dale, a stunning view, a pint in a country pub, a cup of Yorkshire tea and cake, or something more challenging, there's plenty to go at here.

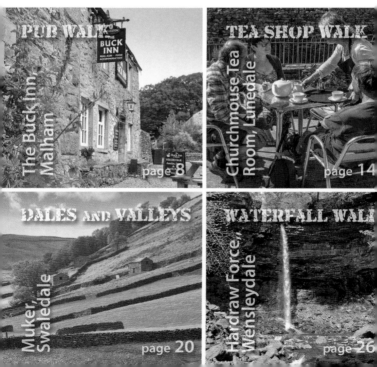

PUB WALK

The Buck Inn, Malham

page 8

TEA SHOP WALK

Churchmouse Tea Room, Lunedale

page 14

DALES AND VALLEYS

Muker, Swaledale

page 20

WATERFALL WALK

Hardraw Force, Wensleydale

page 26

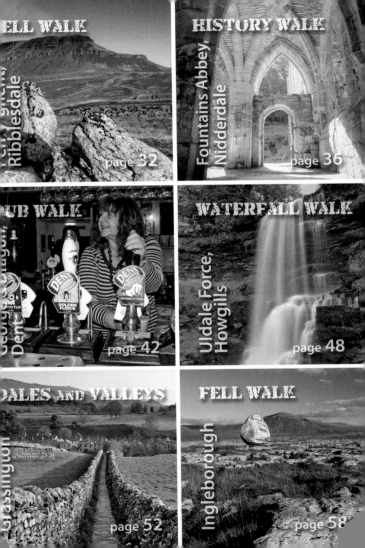

FELL WALK

...., Ribblesdale

page 32

HISTORY WALK

Fountains Abbey, Nidderdale

page 36

PUB WALK

George & Dragon, Dent

page 42

WATERFALL WALK

Uldale Force, Howgills

page 48

DALES AND VALLEYS

Grassington

page 52

FELL WALK

Ingleborough

page 58

Tall delphiniums edge the cobbled forecourt outside the Buck Inn

The Buck Inn Malham

Tackle Malham's rivers and moor before reaching the spectacular twins of Gordale Scar and Malham Cove

What to expect:
Good paths and tracks, some boggy moorland, several short climbs

Distance/time: 10 kilometres/6¼ miles. Allow 3-4 hours

Start/finish: Malham village car park (pay & display)

Grid ref: SD 900 627

Ordnance Survey Map: Explorer OL2 Yorkshire Dales: Southern & Western areas: *Whernside, Ingleborough & Pen-y-ghent*

The Pub: The Buck Inn, Malham, near Skipton, North Yorkshire BD23 4DA | 01729 830317 | www.thebuckmalham.co.uk

Walk outline: The walk accompanies the lively headwaters of the River Aire south before rising on rough paths via Hanlith Moor to Weets Top and a panoramic view over North Yorkshire to distant Bowland and Pendle Hill. Wind then to the mouth of stunning Gordale Scar, before the awesome Malham Cove offers a memorable finale.

At the heart of the village, The Buck Inn *was rebuilt from a coaching inn in 1874 to serve Victorian visitors to the natural wonders of the area. Today's patrons are a mix of ramblers and cavers exchanging banter in the convivial Hikers Bar and families relaxing in the logfire-warmed, panelled lounge.*

The
Buck Inn
at Malham

HIKERS BAR

Families, Dogs
&
Muddy Boots

All Welcome

Welcoming sign

▶ The Buck Inn at a glance

Open: Daily, 12 noon-8.30pm
Brewery/company: Free house
Real ales: Beers from Wensleydale, Timothy Taylor and Theakston breweries
Food: Daily 12 noon-3pm & 6pm-9pm; a strong menu of Dales-sourced ingredients – try the Malham & Masham Pie
Rooms: Twelve en-suite rooms
Outside: Patio; tables to front overlook the beck
Children & dogs: Children welcome, dogs allowed in Hikers Bar

More pub walks ...

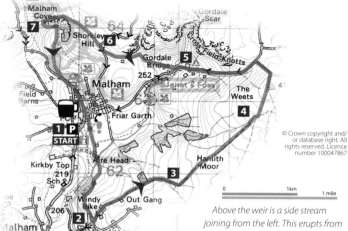

0   1km

1 mile

The Walk

1. Walk downstream alongside **Malham Beck**, water to your right. You're on the **Pennine Way**; the well-trodden path soon reaches a bend near a ruinous barn. Bear right off this bend on the path for 'Hanlith', still the Pennine Way. Possibly muddy pasture leads to **Black Hole Bridge** over **Gordale Beck**. Beyond here the path climbs easily uphill to the first of a number of gates to be used, one well-hidden beneath an ash tree at a wall-end. Down to your right the beck is harvested by a **weir** to fill some trout ponds.

Above the weir is a side stream joining from the left. This erupts from nearby **Aire Head Spring**, *where the waters of the beck which occasionally flows above Malham Cove re-appear from their underground meanderings. This is the same River Aire that flows through Leeds, en-route to the North Sea via the Humber Estuary.*

At a walled corner above a wooded bank and beyond a field gate the 'Pennine Way' is signed left. Follow this direction, gradually peeling away from the wall to use a gate above a converted barn. In a further 75 metres a handgate leads into a tarred lane at a sharp bend here at the top of **Hanlith**.

2. Turn uphill, swinging up this lane past the houses and barns at **Town**

Three walkers inspect medieval Weets Cross

Head, immediately past which the route becomes a rough walled track called **Windy Pike Lane**. This undulates across the hillside, gaining height imperceptibly as ever-better views across the vale to the limestone hills, scars and cliffs above Malham offer a superb horizon.

3. Beyond a sharp-left bend the track reaches a gate into access land at the end of **Hanlith Moor**. For the first 200 metres the continuing track is obvious, but it soon peters out amidst the tussocky — and often boggy — moor.

Your target is the distinct low hilltop slightly-right, capped by a black-looking notch. Choose a way just right of this direction and you'll presently join a line of wall coming up from your right; continue to a gate at the walled corner.

These reedy moors are brimming with wildlife. In spring the marshy flushes are bursting with frog spawn. Look for the tumbling flight of lapwings, or 'peewits' and listen for the mournful cry of the curlew. If you're lucky you may also see a diminutive merlin hunting insects or spot a daylight-hunting short-eared owl.

Walkers on the limestone pavement above Malham Cove

4. Walk from the gate to the fingerpost 100 metres away; here turn left up the good track to a gateway near the 'trig' pillar at **Weets Top**. Commanding views all-round are the reward for this easy climb. The way down is along the gated, walled track beside the weather-worn **Weets Cross**.

The cross is a medieval monastic waymarker, guiding travellers on Fountains Abbey's vast sheep estate here. Only the base is original; the current cross shaft may have been moved from a nearby location.

The track drops to a tarred lane. Turn left and walk down to the sharp-left bend beyond **Gordale House Farm**. The well-made path into **Gordale Scar** is to the right here (extra one kilometre return).

5. The onward route is just round the corner and to the right over the old bridge, signed for 'Malham Cove'. The wallside path rises, offering great views into **Gordale Scar**. At one point a corner handgate puts the wall on your left, soon passing a stone barn. The path now curves right below wires to a lane.

6. Cross right to a ladder-stile and ahead on a stony track. In 300 metres drift left on a grassy track that heads for a distant fingerpost beside a wall. Beyond here

Malham Cove comes into view. The huge semicircle of cliff is topped by a serrated limestone pavement; beautiful, but difficult walking — and remember to keep well back from the edge.

7. At the far side locate the handgate and join the stepped path down into the valley. Follow the sandy path back to **Malham**, to complete the walk. ♦

Underground streams

Malham Cove's stunning curved cliff was created by a vast Niagara-like waterfall as glacial ice-sheets melted around 50-80,000 years ago. Strangely, the seasonal stream that flows well above the cove isn't the same one that appears from the base; the waters supplying this sink into the limestone moor about two kilometres northwest of the cove. Oddly, distant Aire Head Spring receives the waters from above the cove.

The agony of choice at the Churchmouse deli counter

Churchmouse Tea Room

An easy walk across farmland and parkland overlooking the valley of the River Lune

What to expect:
Quiet lanes and fields, riverside, mainly level walking

Distance/Time: 8 kilometres/ 5 miles. Allow 3 hrs

Start: .Village Hall car park, New Road, Barbon

Grid ref: SD 629 823

Ordnance Survey Map: OL2 Yorkshire Dales Southern and Western areas, *Whernside, Ingleborough & Pen-y-ghent*

Tea Room: Churchmouse Tea Room, New Road, Barbon LA6 2LL | 015242 76224 | www.churchmousecheeses.com

Walk outline: The walk leaves Barbon and goes southwards across fields below Barbon Low Fell. Passing through the hamlets of Fell Garth, Hole House, and Langthwaite the route crosses the old Roman Road to reach Casterton. The way swings northwards near the valley bottom, and skirts Gildard Hill, before the River Lune comes into view. Finally, walk along Barbon Beck and back into the village to the Churchmouse Tea Room.

Opening in 2013, the vision for the Churchmouse was to create a 'hub' for local people alongside the pub and the church; a focus for local people to come together in different ways.

Community café

▶ Churchmouse Tea Room at a glance

Open: 08.30 – 16.30 Monday – Saturday; 08.30-15.30 Sunday

Food and Specialities: A village store, fully-licensed café and deli all rolled into one. Speciality cheeses, light lunches and lunchtime specials, locally made cakes, tray bakes, and fresh scones. Try the coffee and walnut or lemon cakes made in the village, or the locally sourced products such as Morecambe Bay shrimps, and Brian Blessed Cheese

Beverages: Speciality teas, Kirkabi Espresso coffee blend from Kirkby Lonsdale, hot chocolate with Belgian chocolate drops, wine and local ales

Dogs: Covered and heated outdoor terrace for dog-owners

More tea shop walks ...

The Walk

1. From the **car park**, turn left into the village passing the **Churchmouse Tea Room** on the right. At the **war memorial**, turn right passing the **Barbon Inn** on your right and the church on your left. Take the footpath on your right signposted 'Underfell'. Walk across the field to a gate to the right of a telegraph pole. Turn left and after 30 metres turn right to cross the field to the left of the house ahead.
Turn right along

the lane, and after some 100 metres take the footpath on the left signposted 'Fell Garth'. After a **small copse**, bear left up to a stile and turn left along a farm track which swings right into beautiful **parkland**. Keep straight ahead along the line of a collapsed wall and ascend the bank. Soon, the imposing **Whelprigg House** (built in 1834 in the Jacobean style) comes into view. Keep ahead, below the house to a fence stile.

2. Cross the driveway of Whelprigg House and continue generally southwards across four fields through field gates (no footpath markers) to arrive at **Fell Garth**. Cross the lane and a **footbridge** signposted 'Langthwaite'. Cross the next field and at the path junction, bear right to pass the tennis court of **Hole House**.

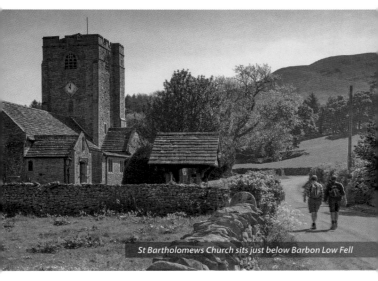

St Bartholomews Church sits just below Barbon Low Fell

Keep ahead, southwards across the next two fields to reach a **bridleway** just beyond **Langthwaite**. Turn right and descend on a tarmac drive for some 400 metres to a road.

This road is on the line of the main Roman road from Manchester to Carlisle via Ribchester. The equivalent of today's M6!

Go straight on under a **railway bridge** and enter the village of **Casterton**. Just before the **church**, turn right to arrive at the **main Kirkby Lonsdale/Sedbergh road**.

Casterton Girls School was founded in 1823 as a Clergy Daughters' School. Charlotte and Emily Bronte were pupils, when the school was at Cowan Bridge. In 2016, it became the Junior section of Sedburgh Public School.

3. Cross over, following a footpath sign and in 50 metres, turn right at a house called '**Beckside**'. Follow the footpath signs through to the school **playing fields**. Go straight on with an all-weather pitch on your left. Follow the path round to the left to cross a **small valley**, bear right at a path junction to

Meandering up the River Lune in high summer

pass an imposing house, **The Grange**, on the right. Immediately after a **walled garden** on the left, turn left. Keep ahead, skirting the **wood** on the left. At the next path junction at a corner of the wood, turn right. At the end of the wood, keep ahead across a large field, generally northwards, with great views of the **River Lune**. **Underley Hall** *is the superb Victorian mansion across the river on your left. The Underley Estate farms and manages 4,500 acres of Lonsdale.* Keep ahead across three large fields to reach a small lane.

4. Turn left down the lane and just before a **bridge**, turn left, and then bear left across **parkland** to reach the **riverside**. Follow the river upstream to reach a lovely **old stone bridge**. Pass under the right hand arch and continue along the riverside for some 600 metres. The path then leaves the riverbank to cross a field to a lane at **Low Beckfoot**. Turn left keeping ahead at the next junction to reach a small bridge over **Barbon Beck** at **Beckfoot Farm**.

5. Turn right through a gate signposted 'Hodge Bridge'. Follow this path keeping the beck to your right. The path crosses a **golf course**. Follow the yellow markers and do not cross any of the bridges on the golf course. A kilometre beyond

Beckfoot Farm, the path meets a road at the historic **Hodge Bridge**.

The 18th century bridge is on the old turnpike from Kirkby Lonsdale to Sedbergh — originally a packhorse route.

6. Turn right over the bridge and then turn left to walk into Barbon. Turn right at the war memorial to reach **The Churchmouse Tea Shop** to complete the walk ◆

River Lune

The River Lune (archaically 'Loyne') is 85 kilometres/53 miles long. It begins in the Howgill Fells at St Helen's Well, near Ravenstonedale, and meets the Irish Sea near Lancaster. The Lune Valley has three parts. The Northern part toTebay is called 'Lunesdale', the central part is the spectacular 'Lune Gorge' through which the M6 and the West Coast Railway line run, and the broad and lush southern part is known as 'Lonsdale' — and which features in this walk.

Swaledale's distinctive walled fields, stone barns and wildflower meadows

Muker Swaledale

Two authentic vernacular villages are linked by parading first above and then alongside the lovely River Swale

What to expect:
Meadow and riverside paths; quiet roads

Distance/time: 10.5 kilometres/ 6½ miles. Allow 3¾ hours

Start: National Park pay & display car park, off Guning Lane, Muker

Grid ref: SD 910 978

Ordnance Survey Map: Explorer OL30 *Yorkshire Dales, Northern & Central areas*

After the walk: The Farmer's Arms and Village Teashop and Stores in Muker; Ghyllfoot Tearoom in Gunnerside

Walk outline

This is a walk of two distinct parts. An elevated daleside road is joined after an initial foray through the delightful Muker meadows. The quietest possible tarmac strip leads scenically to Gunnerside, with an option to cut the walk short via Ivelet Bridge. The return leg keeps to the low meadows, with their jealously guarded heritage herbage.

Swaledale

For all the Yorkshire Dales' scenic unity, no two Dales are alike. Swaledale is narrower than most, with lots to excite eager, questing eyes. Between Muker and Keld, the great 'island' hill of Kisdon is something of a physical curiosity, the valley road and river parting company here. At the end of the last Ice Age, a glacial moraine blocked the original River Swale, diverting it through the present eastern gorge. No doubt hugely influenced by the National Park, the farms and villages along the length of the dale's corridor have retained their vernacular integrity — and a wonderful greenness pervades every casual glance.

Muker

More dales & valleys walks ...

The Walk

1. Cross **Muker Bridge**, straddling **Straw Beck**, to enter the village of **Muker**. Turn up by the **Literary Institute** with its ornate gable-end. The cul-de-sac road leads past **Swale Farm** to a footpath signposted 'Gunnerside & Keld'. The path becomes a flag-paved way that rounds a field barn and advances, via squeeze stiles with their own wicket-gates, through **hay meadows**.

The scent from the meadows, with their unique herbal blend, is intoxicating. No appreciation of Swaledale can be complete without at least once inhaling its sweet perfume. Seen at their best from late May to mid-July, these species-rich meadows are one of the most treasured floral wonders of the Dales, accorded SSSI status. The flagstone paving keeps walkers firmly off the grass.

Coming to the broad, boulder-strewn **River Swale**, turn right — signposted 'FP Gunnerside' — to cross the **Ramps Holme footbridge**.

2. Steps to the left lead onto a track, along which you turn right. The track becomes a metalled road but remains unenclosed. Ascending further, it provides a lovely outlook over the **Muker meadows**. *Its elevation enables walkers to gaze down on the twisting, stony course of the Swale and survey the many laithes, or barns, that seem to occupy every field. The road gives a wonderful sense of freedom with uninhibited views.*

Two miles into the walk, after passing under **Cock Crow Scar** and above **Calvert Houses**, attention is drawn to the Oxnop valley across the dale. The name means 'the valley where plough oxen were kept'. Today, **Swaledale** *looks totally pastoral, but there was a time when*

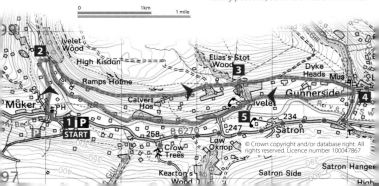

Wildflowers flourish in Swaledale's rich limestone meadows

some of the land was tilled, with oats a predominate crop to feed the horses.

3. Arriving at the junction above the **Ivelet Beck** re-entrant, you may cut the walk short, splicing it almost in two, by turning right, down to **Ivelet Bridge**. But the lure of Gunnerside's tearoom might be enough to hold your resolve to follow the full walk. In which case, keep left, crossing the road-bridge and cattle-grid in the dip. Rising from **Shoregill Head**, the road then sustains its scenic outlook as it drops gently into **Gunnerside**. (The Ghyllfoot Tearoom is beyond the Gunnerside Beck bridge.)

The village-name reflects Viking roots, composed of the Norse personal name 'Gunnar' and a reference to his 'summer shieling or home'.

Above the village and out of sight in the upper reaches of Gunnerside Gill are extensive remains of lead mines. Exploited principally during the 18th and 19th centuries, the scene is laid waste now, nature recovering the ground painfully slowly. The rich veins of lead (galena) were revealed by prospectors damming watercourses. When released, the resulting body of water would scour the slopes, forming grooved hillsides known as

A sea of buttercups colours Swaledale's walled fields and slopes

hushes. The term is an onomatopoeic representation of the whooshing sound of these sudden bursts of water. Now all is silent and a new hush prevails.

4. The walk departs Gunnerside by heading right from the green. The village road leads past the Methodist-maintained school at **Flatlands** to where the Ivelet footpath is indicated on a wicket-gate. A confined path emerges from the community into pasture at a squeeze stile. Traverse the fields by two stiles and a field-gate. After the next squeeze stile, the path rises beside a fence above a river-eroded bank. Continue through a succession

of squeeze stiles, passing behind a field-barn. Three wicket-gates on and the path dips through a dell over a **footbridge** and climbs into the hamlet of **Ivelet**.

5. Turn down the road to **Ivelet Bridge**, entering the meadow at the wicket gate before the bridge — signposted 'FP Muker'. The path starts beside the river but then heads straight on to a wall-top wicket-gate up from the water's edge. After that, it passes through hand gates to approach the river again. Coming down a track ramp, cross the fence-stile and follow the river to the next squeeze stile. Path signs usher walkers across

the next field and, by further wall stiles, past **Ramps Holme**. *The ex-farmstead translates as 'the meadow where wild garlic grows', although there is no sign of this pungent plant today.* The path leads on to re-cross **Ramps Holme footbridge**, from where you retrace your steps into **Muker** to complete the walk. ♦

Barns, or 'Laithes'

The first-time visitor to upper Swaledale will be taken by the sheer number of barns, liberally sprinkled in almost every walled field. Locals still call them by their traditional name: 'laithes'. They harmonise with the setting so beautifully, but their purpose was very down to earth: to provide a loft store of hay gathered in the immediate pasture and a ground floor shippon where cattle were tethered during the winter months.

Hardraw Force is reached through a pub garden

Hardraw Force Wensleydale

Find England's longest single-drop waterfall in the back garden of a fine Dales' pub

What to expect:
Tracks, lanes and field paths; marshy in places

Distance/time: 9.5 kilometres/ 6 miles. Allow 3 hours

Start/finish: Hawes National Park car park (pay & display)

Grid ref: SD 875 898

Ordnance Survey Map: Explorer OL30 Yorkshire Dales: Northern & Central areas: *Wensleydale & Swaledale*

After the walk: Teashops and inns in Hawes

Walk outline

From the Wensleydale market town of Hawes, the Pennine Way is joined, crossing the River Ure before striking through pasture to Hardraw hamlet. The sublime Hardraw Force is reached via the Green Dragon pub's back garden (fee payable) before tracks and field paths meander to Appersett. Join a lane beside the lively Widdale Beck, where smaller falls tumble near the old railway viaduct. Easy moorland roads and footpaths return to Hawes.

Hardraw Force

Hawes is renowned for its Wensleydale Cheese Creamery, which was famously revived by employees and locals following its corporate closure in 1992. The village is also situated near the meeting of half-a-dozen major and minor dales, the becks of which cascade down from the enclosing high fells over countless waterfalls.

This walk visits the most famous of these falls, hidden in a gorge behind a sublime village pub; whilst others tumble prettily through village centres. Magnificent views of the northern Dales accompany the walk, with stunning panoramas over this quiet corner of the National Park.

River Ure roots

More waterfall walks ...

The Walk

1. From the eastern end of the town's one-way system near the **Ropemakers' Works**, take the road for 'Muker and Industrial Estate'. Look for a Pennine Way fingerpost here. Cross the former railway before slipping into the industrial estate road.

Look to the right for the **Pennine Way**, and follow it across fields to regain the road near **Haylands Bridge**. Cross

this and, in another 200 metres, go left on the field path for 'Hardraw'. This well-walked path slinks across several pastures, rejoining the Pennine Way on the approach to **Hardraw** village and the nearby **Green Dragon Inn**.

The bar of this delightful pub is also the entrance to the waterfall! **Hardraw Force** is a thin dagger plummeting over 30 metres into a great limestone cove dripping with ferns and mosses. *The highest single-drop, overground falls in England, Hardraw was used as a location for the film* Robin Hood, Prince of Thieves. *The enchanting approach up a wooded chasm reveals a network of paths first developed by a Victorian entrepreneur. His 'improvements' included repairing the lip of the waterfall, which fell off in a violent storm-surge in 1899.*

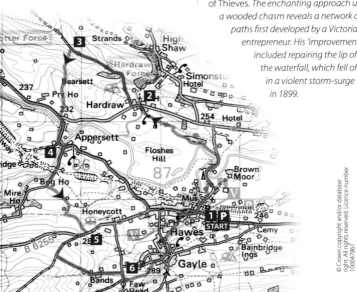

Hardraw Force plummets 30 metres into a vast limestone cove

2. Return from the falls, turn right from the inn and cross the bridge. Immediately past the **old school**, turn right on the **Pennine Way** up a walled track that curls above woodland.

Magnificent views open out ahead to Great Shunner Fell, one of the highest points on the Pennine Way, whilst behind you is a grand panorama across higher Wensleydale.

Remain on the track as it levels out beyond the woods. Around 600 metres later, look for a gate on the left, signposted to 'New Bridge'.

3. Walk beside the wall down boggy pasture and cross a corner stile. The way now drops more steeply and slightly left, gaining the first of a line of wayposts guiding the route across rough pasture, heading just left of dome-topped Dodd Fell. Cross further stiles and aim well to the right of the **old barn** and sycamores to reach a road junction. Go left on the main Hawes road, cross the **New Bridge** over the **River Ure** and then slip right into a footpath parallel to the road. Stay with this to the bridge at the edge of **Appersett hamlet**.

Superb views over drystone-walled Wensleydale from the fells above Hardraw Force

4. Turn right off the bridge up the tarred lane, rising gently above **Widdale Beck**. Noisy **waterfalls** mark its passage beneath the railway viaduct, a popular spot with abseilers. As the lane levels at a righthand-bend, take the path on the left, signposted to 'Ashes'. Head across the pasture on a faint track, go over a stone stile and drop through a shallow valley past a barn to a fingerpost near a ruinous lime kiln. Go right, through the higher handgate and then up the slope to a wall-gap. Turn hard-left, walking above the wall-line. Bend right with the field elbow, tracing the wall on your left to a gate into a lane.

5. Walk uphill to the nearby fork; then head along a rough track called **Cam Road**. In 400 metres, opposite a hut, turn left on another walled track and remain with this past farms to a T-junction.

6. Turn uphill to find the waymarked **Pennine Way**, signed to your left for 'West End'. Cross the hay meadows on a thin path through several handgates to another fingerpost. Take the path for 'Gayle', soon reaching a village lane. Turn right and wind through **Gayle** to the bridge over **Gayle Beck**.

Waterfalls cascade through the village and a leat leads to the nearby Victorian sawmill.

Turn back from the bridge and bend right for Hawes. At the slope-foot take the **Pennine Way** right, passing below the creamery to reach **Hawes church**. Turn right on the path to the town where stepped waterfalls crash between the buildings, to complete the walk. ◆

Wensleydale cheese

Hawes was granted a market charter as late as 1699, replacing tiny Askrigg as the market centre for higher Wensleydale. The market thrived and continues to do so. Here, too, are the remarkable 200-year-old Ropemaker's Works, and the creamery where genuine Wensleydale cheese is produced. Even today it's still made using the original recipe first developed by monks at Jervaulx Abbey back in the 12th century.

Pen-y-ghent rises above the autumn fells

Pen-y-ghent Ribblesdale

Essentially a simple hill-walk, yet brimming with the geological essence of the National Park

What to expect:
Constructed fell paths; worn-earth fell paths; stone tracks

Distance/time: 9.5 kilometres/ 6 miles. Allow 4¼ hours

Start/finish: National Park pay & display car park in Horton-in-Ribblesdale

Grid ref: SD 807 725

Ordnance Survey Map: Explorer OL2 Yorkshire Dales: Southern & Western areas: *Whernside, Ingleborough & Pen-y-ghent*

After the walk: Pen-y-ghent Café, Blind Beck Tearooms, Golden Lion and Crown Hotel, all in Horton

Walk outline

Go climb your mountain and be chuffed you did. Of the beetling Three Peaks, this is the Ringo Starr, beating its own drum. An up-and-over climb, it incorporates lovely contact with limestone country features, particularly if a moment is given to carefully view the impressive Hull Pot. The walk ends with a scenic stroll down Horton Scar Lane. It's an expedition of the well trammelled kind, but fabulously worthy for all that.

Pen-y-ghent

Pen-y-ghent is a very commanding presence in upper Ribblesdale. The distinctive cap of millstone grit rests on a sequence of Carboniferous limestone beds, the whole resisting the weathering onslaught of ice to give an eye-catching must-climb headland above the village of Horton-in-Ribblesdale. The under-moor of 'hollow' limestone is riddled with caverns where streams are lost to sunlight, invariably emerging as gushing watercourses where they encounter the impervious Silurian shales in the valley floor of Ribblesdale.

Hull pot

More fell walks …

The Walk

1. Turn right out of the car park and follow the footway beside the **B6479**, passing the **Pen-y-ghent café** (Tourist Information Centre). After the **church**, cross the road bridge spanning **Douk Ghyll** and bear left along the side road.

2. The road rises to **Brackenbottom Farm**. At the first barn, heed the signpost 'Pen-y-ghent summit' directing you left via hand-gates. Embark on a steady pasture climb with a drystone wall on the left. Two modest limestone rock-steps lead to a wall-stile; otherwise, it's hand-gates and pitching to the ridge-top to join the **Pennine Way**.

3. Turn up left on a stone-pitched trail towards the southern 'nose' of Pen-y-ghent. The path naturally veers right as the upper tier of limestone looms. This rock hazard is taken by small, natural steps. The path winds upwards to the topmost gritstone tier where a genuine rock-step demands

steady handling. The path eases onto the **summit of Pen-y-ghent** where you find a small **cairn and OS column** at 694 metres/2,277 feet.

4. Cross the adjacent wall-stile and walk away from the wall on a trail which drifts easily down the fellside, veering from northwest to north along the edge. The path drops to a footpath sign with a limestone cliff ahead.

The crag is a precious habitat of the rare and delicate Alpine purple saxifrage.

5. The gravel path leads down to a gate/ladder-stile. After some 400 metres, watch for a pasture path veering back left. This is a spur route, allowing you to cautiously inspect **Hunt Pot**, a deep

The wallside path from Brackenbottom looking towards Pen-y-ghent

pothole consuming the watercourse draining the fell's western slopes. Regain the trail and, after a double ladder-stile/ gate, you reach a gate giving access to **Horton Scar Lane**.

6. Before setting off down the lane, you are encouraged to make a there-and- back visit to inspect **Hull Pot** — by following the track right for 400 metres.

A tiny beck enters the limestone under- world at Hull Pot, spilling 20 metres into a great hollow, a collapsed cavern.

From Hull Pot, backtrack and follow Horton Scar Lane south, all the way to the **village** street. Go right to return to the car park and complete the walk. ♦

'Yorkshire Three Peaks' challenge

Horton-in-Ribblesdale has become synonymous with the Yorkshire Three Peaks Walk, taking in the summits of Pen-y-ghent, Whernside and Ingleborough at the head of Ribblesdale. While many see it as a race, others see sufficient challenge just in completing the 38km/ 23 mile walk. The Yorkshire Dales National Park runs a voluntary 'Friends of the Three Peaks' project, the proceeds of which go towards the upkeep of paths along the route.

Accomplished Gothic vaulting at Fountains Abbey

Fountains Abbey Nidderdale

An atmospheric walk across two medieval estates with a fine viewpoint over Nidderdale

What to expect:
Tracks and quiet lanes across farmland and through woods

Distance/time: 11 kilometres / 6¾ miles. Allow 3½-4 hours

Start: West Gate car park, Fountains Abbey, about 5 kilometres west of Ripon

Grid ref: SE 271 682

Ordnance Survey Map: Explorer 298 Nidderdale: *Fountains Abbey, Ripon, and Pateley Bridge*

After the walk: Abbey Tea Rooms, Fountains Abbey HG4 3DY | 01765 600158 | www.nationaltrust.org.uk/fountains-abbey

Walk outline

This superb walk links two important medieval sites in North Yorkshire — Fountains Abbey of the Cistercian Order and a fortified moated manor house, Markenfield Hall, a rare survival. In monastic times, their estates adjoined so the whole of this walk is on land previously owned either by the abbey or the Markenfield estate. The route is through woods, quiet lanes and field paths with a gentle climb to the chapel on How Hill.

A medieval landscape

Rarely does one have the opportunity to walk through a landscape essentially unchanged since the Middle Ages. Fountains Abbey was founded in 1132 by Benedictine monks who preferred the simpler life of the Cistercian Order. By 1539, when Henry VIII shut down the monasteries, the abbey owned 500 acres, with much more in the Dales and Lake District.

Romanesque arcade

The owner of Markenfield Hall got a licence to crenellate in 1310 but, because of the family's involvement in the pro-Catholic Rising of the North in 1569, his property was confiscated and handed to Thomas Egerton who never lived in the Hall — which devolved to a rented farmhouse.

More history walks ...

Yorkshire Dales

The Walk

1. From the **West Gate car park** at **Fountain's Abbey**, turn right on the road and then bear left at a fork signed 'Markington'. After 200m turn left through a gate. The ancient **Abbey Wall** is to your right and views over the Abbey and Fountains Hall on the left.

The Abbey Wall originally stood at nearly four metres high and is said to be the largest remaining monastic wall in Britain. The late Elizabethan Fountains Hall was built partly from the Abbey's stone. The Duke and Duchess of York (later George VI and Queen Elizabeth) often stayed here as guests of the Marquess of Ripon.

Continue past a pond on your left, known as **Robin Hood's Well**. Around 500 metres from the beginning of the path, go through a gate and, at a **copse**, turn right. **Hill House Farm** is on your left as the track swings left over a **stone bridge** and through a gate.

2. Follow the waymarks through the **farmyard** to a gate and continue along the track with a hedge on your right. When the hedge ends, bear left across the field to a gate into a wood. 100 metres later, you pass an **old archway in the Abbey Wall**.

This archway, into Mackershaw Deer Park, was part of 'Mackershaw Lodge', a gatehouse and estate worker's house in the C19th.

Continue on this wide track for about 750 metres, ignoring tracks downhill to the left, until you ascend to leave the wood. Follow the **line of ancient trees** to **Whitcliffe Lane**.

3. Turn right and continue for about

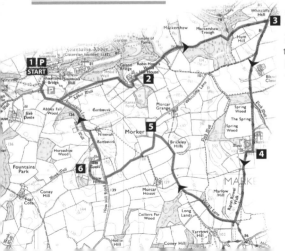

Markenfield Hall features a superb Tudor gatehouse

500 metres until you reach a **cattle grid** into open fields with a farm, **Bland Close**, to the left. Keep straight ahead across two fields where the path is joined from the left by the old **deer park wall**. Cross this ancient wall through a stile and over a stream. The imposing **Markenfield Hall** comes into view which you reach by gently ascending across two fields. Walk across the **car park** to the **gatehouse**. *Note the black swans in the moat, a tradition at Markenfield.*

Although not open to the public, from this Tudor gatehouse you can see the internal arrangement of stabling (left), domestic quarters (right), and the chapel (originally the Great Hall) straight ahead. The powerful Markenfield family were brought to their knees by their involvement in the Rising of the North. It was in this courtyard that a large contingent of the Rising mustered in November 1569 under the banner of 'The Five Wounds of Christ'. They heard Mass in the Chapel and set out for London. However, the Rising was routed and Sir Thomas de Markenfield fled to the Low Countries, dying in poverty in 1592.

Fountains Abbey is dramatically floodlit after dark

4. From the gatehouse, take the way-marked path between **farm buildings**. The route, southwards along a grass track, crosses three fields. In the third field, bear right to a stile. Turn right into **Strait Lane**, rather overgrown at first.

Strait Lane is an ancient 'holloway', probably medieval, following the deer park wall, and heading for Fountains Abbey.

After a kilometre, the lane emerges into a field. Keep to the edge of two fields with a hedge on the right. Bear right across a third field to a gate. In the next field corner go through a gap in the hedge and continue with a hedge on your right to reach **Whitcliffe Lane**.

5. Turn left and walk south, then south eastwards towards How Hill. At a road junction, turn left and, after 75 metres, turn right through a gate to climb **How Hill** to the former **Chapel of St Michael de Monte**.

A chantry chapel built around 1200 and then rebuilt by Abbot Huby in the early C16th. Thought to be a medieval place of pilgrimage, since it is possible to see York Minster, Selby Abbey, and Ripon Cathedral from here. To the west is an Abbey fish pond in the nearby woods enclosed by the 'Monk Wall', vestiges of which are still apparent.

6. Head downhill towards red-roofed **How Hill Cottages** to meet the road again and turn left. This lane follows the course of the **Monk Wall** back to the car park , to complete the walk. ◆

But before you go, make sure you leave enough time to visit the Abbey and Studley Royal.

The monks are still here

Archaeological research, using ground-penetrating radar, has located more than 500 graves of monks and lay brothers east of the abbey church. The graves show a 'bunk-bed' formation with up to four bodies separated by stone partitions within the same grave. This supports the theory that the community believed in 'corporeal resurrection' whereby a person's physical remains would rise from the grave on the Day of Judgement.

THE DENT BREWERY TAP

Sunlight illuminates the wood panelled interior of the George & Dragon, in Dent

George & **Dragon** Dentdale

Astonishing views to the Howgill Fells and a tranquil riverside return to Dent's quaint old village lanes

What to expect:
Good, maybe muddy paths and tracks. Steady climb to start

Distance/time: 8 kilometres/ 5 miles. Allow 2½ -3 hours

Start/finish: Car park (pay & display) in Dent village

Grid ref: SD 704 871

Ordnance Survey Map: Explorer OL2 Yorkshire Dales: *Southern & Western areas: Whernside, Ingleborough & Pen-y-ghent*

The Pub: The George & Dragon, Main Street, Dent, Cumbria LA10 5QL | 015396 25256 | www.georgeanddragondent.co.uk

Walk outline: A lane rising from Dent's memorable mix of cobbles, cottages and ginnels soon narrows to a steep, wooded track beside waterfalls before gaining an old moorland roadway curling across Towns Fell. Marvellous views across Dentdale reward before a bridlepath drops into Deepdale and a riverside return on the Dales Way to Dent.

The George & Dragon *commands a corner at the heart of the quaint village. This traditional pub, all panels and log fires, appeals to all-comers, from weary ramblers to sports fans and family groups, with a suite of rooms in which to quaff Dentdale-brewed real ales. The nearby Sun Inn is also a treat.*

Sun Inn sign

▶ **The George & Dragon at a glance**

Open: Daily, 10.30am-11pm; 12 noon-10.30pm Sundays
Brewery/company: Dent Brewery
Real ales: Dent Brewery beers plus guests
Food: Daily, 12 noon-2.30pm and 6pm-9pm. A quality, wide-ranging menu; some dishes cooked in Dent beers
Rooms: Ten en-suite rooms
Outside: None
Children & dogs: Children and dogs welcome

More pub walks ...

The Walk

1. Choose the road opposite the car park entrance, which climbs past cottages to the village green. Keep ahead up the 'No Through Road'. Beyond a final cottage the lane deteriorates to a stony track, signed as a bridleway to **'Flintergill'**, a terrific, steep wooded cleft.

On the left in just a few metres a side path drops to a slabby riverbed, known locally as **Dancing Flags**. *Local weavers used to spread out their cloth here and 'waulk' it — wash, de-grease and felt the material.*

Return to the track and wind through a gate.

Just a short distance further up the track is a tree with an undercut root system — the **Wishing Tree***. Folklore has it that if you pass through the root-bole gap three times in a clockwise direction you'll be granted a wish; do it widdershins (anticlockwise) and you'll have bad luck!*

The track climbs consistently within the woodland fringe. Immediately before the gate take the chance to divert right to the stone barn.

This old building at **High Ground farmstead** *is packed with old agricultural machinery*

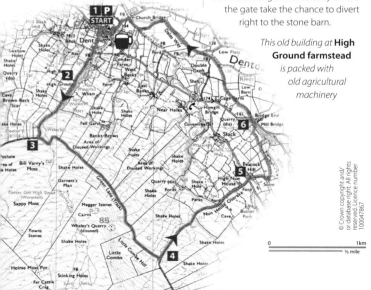

Dent's quaint cobbled streets lead to the old Sun Inn

and implements plus a display of old
photographs of Dentdale's farming
community. Nearby is a restored limekiln.
One of many dotted across the Dentdale
hillsides, it produced lime from roasting
limestone, put to many uses in industry,
farming and household maintenance.

2. Continuing uphill, the woodland
peels away at the next gate; divert right
50 metres to the little knoll to find a
toposcope identifying the highlights
of the extraordinary views from here.
Return to the track and continue up to
a T-junction.

3. Turn left on this old walled track,
called **Occupation Road**.

The walls here are straight in comparison
to the smaller, higgledy-piggledy ancient
fields in the valley. This results from the
Enclosure Acts of the 19th century, when
the common land of the moors was 'taken
in' from the wild by farmers intent on
land improvement. This old droving road
became important access for such farmers
who 'occupied' these intakes of land.

The rutted track undulates across the
fellside, with great views ahead of

The Howgills rise beyond verdant Dentdale

Whernside, one of the famous Three Peaks of the Yorkshire Dales, beloved of geography and geology teachers.

Local geology was an interest of Adam Sedgwick, son of the Vicar of Dent. He became an academic at Cambridge, where his studies in stratigraphy revolutionised geology. One of his students was Charles Darwin.

4. At the next T-junction turn left, a rougher walled track signed for 'Nun House Outrake'.

Here's where the views across Dentdale come into their own. The northern slopes are dissected by short, wooded gills, each plugged by a stone or whitewashed farmhouse at its foot. To your left the shapely upwellings of the Howgill Fells are a study in landscape perfection, draping the horizon like a giant croissant.

Pass by the house at **Nun House**, dropping down the concreted driveway to reach a tarred lane.

5. Cross straight over and use three gates in-series through the farmyard area, continuing down the right edge of a pasture. Turn left through the handgate above the ruined **Scow farmhouse**; the waymarked path falls across the pasture to a handgate. Pass a limekiln and keep above the old wall-

line beyond this, looking for a higher handgate into a continuing pasture. Some 75 metres before a rebuilt cross-wall look right for a road bridge over **Deepdale Beck**; drop to this.

6. Don't cross the bridge; instead look left for the waymarked riverside footpath which now accompanies the beck, then the **River Dee** back to **Dent Bridge**. Turn left to the village. ◆

The 'Terrible knitters'

Dentdale was famed for its knitwear, popular with the military from Napoleonic times onwards. Such was the almost manic speed and skill of the craftspeople that they became known as the 'Terrible knitters' of Dent, a badge of honour worn with pride. The last such knitters both died in 2007, ending a venerable tradition.

Uldale Force is hidden in a remote canyon

Uldale Force Howgill Fells

A challenging approach to a remote series of falls secluded below Baugh Fell at the fringe of the Howgill Fells

What to expect:
Lanes, tracks and narrow paths; some scrambling; marshy sections

Distance/time: 10.5 kilometres/ 6½ miles. Allow 3-4 hours
Start/finish: Layby beside A683 road 200 metres west of Rawthey Bridge, 6 miles north-east of Sedbergh
Grid ref: SD 712 978
Ordnance Survey Map: Explorer OL19 *Howgill Fells & Upper Eden Valley*
After the walk: The Cross Keys Temperance Inn at Cautley, 1 mile south of Rawthey Bridge; pubs, cafés and hotels in Sedbergh

Walk outline

This walk in the western fringe of the National Park follows a narrow lane across Ravenstonedale Common. A sparse quarrymen's path is joined up wooded Rawthey Gill, past a series of lively falls to reach the memorable downfall of Uldale Force. The return follows a reedy bridleway across the side of West Baugh Fell. Perversely, plan to do this walk after a good dry spell, as the paths near Uldale Force are thin and slippery.

Uldale Force

This seldom-visited corner of The Dales—actually in Cumbria—reveals a very unfamiliar countryside. The magnificent Howgill Fells create a memorable horizon. An astonishing series of waterfalls tumble from the heights into wooded gorges and gills, culminating in the matriarch of the system, the memorable Uldale Force, hidden in its remote canyon. Reaching it requires determination and surefootedness; the deceptively easy approach on tranquil lanes is soon replaced by thin, challenging paths etched into the gorge side.

This is the most demanding walk in this book; a richly rewarding exploration of an exquisite, hidden landscape.

More waterfall walks ...

White Green Farm

The Walk

1. Cross **Rawthey Bridge** and take the narrow lane forking right for 'Uldale Fell End'. This rises easily past a few remote farms, soon levelling along the edge of **Ravenstonedale Common**.

To your left is a sweeping view of the Howgill Fells, described by the fellwalker Alfred Wainwright as 'looking like a herd of sleeping elephants'. The dark crags and screes are Cautley Crag, the flank of Great Dummacks. Along with adjoining Calf Fell, it is the highest land in these remote hills. Tumbling down the gash in the hillside here is **Cautley Spout**, *England's highest waterfall which drops in stages over 180 metres.*

2. Turn right on the tarred lane signposted for 'Uldale Head', winding across rushy upland pasture that rises to the heights of looming **Wild Boar Fell**. *A few secluded farms dapple these acres; one at White Green is a poignant, abandoned reminder of times when far more people farmed these uplands.*

3. Where the lane forks, remain on the higher level, passing through a gate into **Uldale**, signed as a bridleway and footpath to 'Grisedale'. The concreted track dips through wooded **Needlehouse Gill**; at the far side, turn right on the fingerposted bridleway for 'Bluecaster', a pleasant wood-edged way carpeted with pinecones. Beyond a gate the track descends to cross a footbridge over the **River Rawthey**.

4. Turn upstream; the track soon deteriorates in quality and width. Roughly a kilometre later, just past a river-edge boulder fall, notice a two-metre high pillar of stones on a ledge up on your right; there are **caverns** behind. About 50 metres beyond, fork right, up the grassy path into **old workings**.

The River Rawthey at Uldale

Continue upstream, now perhaps 30 metres above the river. The thin path, vague in parts, presently crosses the clefts of **two extremely steep gills**. After the second, head downhill into the gorge, picking your way up to **Uldale Force**, secreted in a semicircular embayment.

5. Return to the footbridge. Don't cross it but instead join the stony track angling out of the valley. Remain with this for two kilometres across the flank of the moor, contrasting sharply with the grassy fields opposite.

6. At a lone, low bridleway marker turn right on a track back to **Rawthey Bridge** to complete the walk. ♦

Yorkshire Dales or Lake District?

The River Lune's gorge, which is followed by both the mainline railway and the M6, separates the Yorkshire Dales and Lake District National Parks. It was somehow overlooked when the Park designations were made in the 1950s. But in August 2016, this area of tortuous becks and remote fells—including the northern Howgills, Ravenstonedale, Wild Boar Fell and Great Asby Scar— was added to the Yorkshire Dales National Park.

Narrow Sedber Lane, above Grassington

Grassington Wharfedale

Soothing river scenery and charming villages amid a spacious, authentically Dales pastoral landscap

What to expect:

Riverside paths; field paths; narrow walled lanes; gentle gradients

Distance/time: 7 kilometres/ 5¼ miles. Allow 3 hours

Start/finish: National Park free car park at Linton Falls. If full, try the pay & display car park in Grassington. From Grassington, drop to Linton Falls from the the car park via Sedber Lane

Grid ref: SE 002 633

Ordnance Survey Map: Explorer OL2 Yorkshire Dales: Southern & Western areas: *Whernside, Ingleborough & Pen-y-ghent*

After the walk: Red Lion and village tearoom in Burnsall at the half-way point; choice of venues in Grassington

Walk outline

With Linton Falls as the exciting prelude, intimately observed from a suspension footbridge, wander serenely with the serpentine flow of the Wharfe to Burnsall Bridge. From here, either retrace your steps, or, seeking a sense of perspective on the greater valley setting, traverse the gracious pastureland to the south, via the enchanting little community of Thorpe.

Grassington

Wharfedale has long been a gateway to the glories of the Dales for people with a Yorkshire mill-town perspective — with Grassington an immensely popular day-trip destination. The pastoral nature of the surrounding countryside is embodied in the village name, which means 'the grazing-farm'. There is also evidence of former tilled ground, with strip lynchet terracing of medieval origin, further affirmed by the nearby Saxon village-name of Threshfield, or 'place where corn is threshed'. It was in such places that most of the county's pre-Industrial Revolution population resided, deeply rooted in a productive agricultural economy, later dominated by arduous, but lucrative, lead mining.

Grassington village

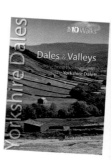

More dale and valley walks ...

The Walk

1. From the car park, walk back to where the **Linton Falls** are signposted right by **Falls House**. Keep right again, by the millstream, avoiding **Little Emily's Bridge**, a quaint packhorse bridge situated on the former Threshfield-to-Linton-Church path. Cross the long **suspension footbridge**, admiring the weirs and the river bursting through the limestone bedrock on the Craven Fault.

This is the fourth bridge to occupy this site. The first, known as the Tin Bridge, was rather crudely constructed in 1814 to give access for workers to the mill. Spellbound by the acoustic agitation, linger as you will.

No doubt you'll not be alone: this place has drawn its admirers from long ages past, being the largest waterfall on the Wharfe. The hydraulic power of the water caused the National Park Authority to consider harnessing the century-old water gate as a hydroelectric plant.

Once across — at the foot of **Sedber Lane** — bear right by the wall-stile and traverse the meadow in harmony with the **Dales Way**, signposted 'Hebden & Burnsall'. The meadow route leads on by a squeeze stile and gated wall-stile, rising as a gravel pathway above the river to a stepped wall-stile. Here it enters a confined road.

2. Go right, passing **Brow Well fisheries** to where the lane ends at a hand-gate.

*Over to the right are some **stepping stones**, a very old crossing point installed for the exclusive benefit of parishioners attending Linton Church.*

The level pathway heads left via a footbridge and then goes through two further hand-gates more intimate with the free-flowing river.

The picturesque pedestrian suspension bridge over the River Wharfe

3. Cross the **suspension footbridge**; the adjacent stepping stones are tempting only when the river is truly low. After a hand-gate, advance to the next excitement: **Loup Scar**, where the river 'loops' beneath a picturesque limestone cliff. Rise and descend onto a walkway at the river's edge. Beyond a metal kissing-gate, the path leads to **Burnsall Bridge** beside the **Red Lion Inn**.

4. Follow the village road right. Rounding a right-hand bend, follow a confined footpath signposted off to the left after 30 metres. This traverses a series of narrow fields via a succession of wall-stiles with a green lane in the midst. Climbing a bank to a further wall-stile, come over the next pasture to cross a stony lane via facing gated wall-stiles.

5. The clear field-path dips through a **shallow gill**. After a wall-stile, advance with a wall on the right and then woodland to a hand-gate. After this, enter a walled green lane which ends at a gate onto a country road.

6. Turn left, descending into **Thorpe** by the **Manor House**. Keep ahead,

Burnsall village, its bridge and riverside sheep pastures

rising from the triangular green by some attractive dwellings to come to a T-junction. Turn left along the road, signposted 'Cycle route 688/unsuitable for HGVs'. This is **Thorpe Lane**, providing a grand view north across Wharfedale. Stride out along the road, traversing the northern slopes of **Elbolton**.

This 'hill of the fairies' is a pudding-shaped hill peppered with caves such as **Navvy Noodle Hole**. **Elbolton Cave**, *which has a narrow entry and an instant drop of 5 metres, was excavated in 1890 revealing the bones of bear, arctic fox, hare and reindeer. In 1920, Arthur Raistrick, the Dales landscape historian, revisited the cave and discovered human burials within stone cists of Late Neolithic and Early Bronze Age.*

7. Leave the road where a narrow walled lane departs right at a hand-gate signposted 'BW to B6160'. The lane winds its way down among the lynchet fields, ending at a hand-gate. Follow the remnant wall part-way down the pasture, slanting half-left to a gate. Then continue to the foot of the hill and a hand-gate onto the **B6160** road.

8. Turn right and walk along the road for 15 metres. Then go left, through the gate. A clear path angles half-left

via a wall-stile to cross the brow by a lone field-barn and then continues to a wall-stile. The path slips past the fixed gate in the corner to enter a short lane by Holme House. This leads onto a road, along which you turn left to return to the Linton Falls car park to complete the walk. ♦

Strip lynchets

Few pastures are ploughed today, but regular lynchet terracing — both up and across slopes — are the result of intensive cultivation from the age of strip farming. Each lynchet would've been horse-ploughed and crops hand-harvested to serve a large local population whose lives were focused on the ebb and flow of the agricultural year. The walk either side of Thorpe encounters these remains within what is now sheep and cattle pasture.

Ingleborough with a huge glacial 'erratic' perched on limestone pavement

Ingleborough Ribblesdale

An abundance of limestone features and an amazing gritstone plateau on the pick of the Yorkshire Three Peaks

What to expect:
Firm tracks; well-maintained fell paths

Distance/time: 15 kilometres/ 9½ miles. Allow 6 hours

Start/finish: National Park pay & display car park in Clapham

Grid ref: SD 745 692

Ordnance Survey Map: Explorer OL2 Yorkshire Dales: Southern & Western areas: *Whernside, Ingleborough & Pen-y-ghent*

After the walk: The New Inn Hotel and Croft Café beside the car park in Clapham

Walk outline

Ingleborough makes for one of the truly great fell days in the National Park. A wooded dale leads by the mouth of Ingleborough Cave through a romantic craggy defile onto the open moor. The walk takes leave of the sub-moor by a paved trail climbing to the high plateau. Coming onto the summit we orbit the scenic edges of this plateau. Escaping east, the walk ventures downhill via a wide expanse of untamable surface limestone. It then comes upon a winding green trail that ultimately reconnects with the Clapdale approach.

Gaping Gill cavern

Ingleborough

This stand alone iconic mountain, rising to 723 metres/2,372 feet, is composed of layers of rock, beautifully revealed during this walk. From the bed of Silurian shales in Clapham, the walker comes quickly to the gleaming white Carboniferous limestone rising above Clapdale to witness a moorland stream consumed by Gaping Gill. Climbing the mountain are dark bands of gritstone, originally formed in an ancient river delta. The daleside scars and semi-dissolved surface plates of limestone were scoured by ancient ice sheets.

More fell walks ...

The Walk

1. Leave the **village car park**, bearing right and then left over the little packhorse-style bridge spanning **Clapdale Beck**. Wend your way up **Riverside**, passing the original editorial home of *The Dalesman* magazine. Passing the **Church Avenue** junction next to **St James' Church**, continue by the **falls** to arrive at the entrance to **Clapdale** proper. **Ingleborough Hall Estate** offers public access for a fee to its private drive beside the lake.

2. Penniless walkers can side-step this Nature Trail by following the lane a bit further to a junction, embarking on the farm track on the right. This bridleway is signposted to 'Ingleborough Cave, Gaping Gill and Ingleborough'. The track has its own scenic merit, rising above the trees to view Thwaite Scars on the far side of Clapdale. Pass through the yard of **Clapdale Farm** and, from the gate at the end, descend naturally into the valley. At a fence-stile, you join forces with the estate drive to arrive at **Ingleborough Cave**.

3. The track goes through a gate and soon the dale constricts. After the next gate, the trail turns a corner and

A track snakes through limestone pavement below Ingleborough

s confronted by the picturesque and
mpressive dry ravine of **Trow Gill**. You
will find the tumble of rocks awkward
as you thread through the tight exit at
ts top. Follow on with a snaking wall in
the dry valley and duly cross the twin
adder-stile.

4. The popular path leads on past two
potholes to reach a fork in the way after
400 metres.

The right-hand track leads to the
shocking, dark hole of **Gaping Gill**,
where **Fell Beck** plunges underground
into a deep cavern the size of a

cathedral. *The utmost caution is required
should you be tempted to step down to get
up close and personal!*

The main route, however, goes left. This
duly sets to work on sections of gravel
and paving slabs to climb the steep
southeast flank of **Little Ingleborough**.
The paving forms **steps** higher up,
passing a large, ragged **cairn** as the crest
is neared.

5. Continue along the comparatively
narrow south ridge. There is a rise and
then one final, more concerted step up
to an **interpretative panel**. The path

A low winter sun colours the trees below a silhouetted Ingleborough

angles up to draw you to the centre of the table-top.

A stroll orbiting the perimeter of the plateau, where there is evidence of ramparts, is a must, although most settle on the **summit cross-wall** for a wind-lee break.

The view northwest to Ribblehead, the famous viaduct, and beyond Whernside to the distant Howgills all give plenty of good reason to stay and enjoy your time after the effort of the long ascent.

6. Exit the plateau via the narrow stony edge of **Swine's Tail** at the north-western corner of the summit. The popular trail swings down and across the long southern slopes of **Simon Fell Breast**, heading for a twin ladder-stile. Beyond this, walk beside a wall and past a roofless **shooting box** to cross a **ford** and pass through a hand-gate.

7. As the path forks, hold to the right-hand green way. There are old **stone grouse butts** nearby. Soon, **limestone pavement** grabs the attention as a green track weaves through a cut passage in the rocks. After crossing the line of a broken wall and shortly after the clints are lost, veer right again, now with the acorn waymarking of the **Pennine Bridleway** as your guide on **Long Scar**.

8. The green way drifts easily down, passing close to a wall corner as it does so. Descend through the pastures and, after the second gate, go through a holding pen. This is followed by a track, but you need to watch for a ladder-stile that enables you to skip over the adjacent wall. Now descend the bank to a further ladder-stile and enter the dry valley directly below **Trow Gill**. From here, retrace your steps through **Clapdale** to complete the walk. ♦

The 'Dalesman'

Clapham was the birthplace of The Dalesman magazine, which has reflected the life of the Dales since 1939. Founder Harry Scott was succeeded by Bill Mitchell MBE. Bill had a 40-year association, mostly as editor, and continues his prodigious output of Dales and Cumbrian books, presently numbering 160! A memorial to Harry, in the form of a wrought-iron gate, is located on the way to the Village Hall from Riverside.

Useful Information

'Welcome to Yorkshire'
This comprehensive website draws together a wealth of information about visiting Yorkshire. **www.yorkshire.com**

Yorkshire Dales National Park
For in-depth information about the National Park, including 'What's on' listings of local events and tourist information. **www.yorkshiredales.org.uk**

Visitor Centres
Many towns in the area have Tourist Information Centres where staff will help with accommodation, heritage and outdoor activities. The main ones are listed here; there are also National Park Centres in some key locations.

Tourist Information Centres

Horton-in-Ribblesdale	01729 860333	horton@ytbtic.co.uk
Ingleton	01524 241049	ingleton@ytbtic.co.uk
Leyburn	01748 828747	ticleyburn@richmondshire.co.uk
Sedbergh	01539 620125	tic@sedbergh.org.uk
Settle	01729 825192	settle@ytbtic.co.uk
Skipton	01756 792809	skipton@ytbtic.co.uk

National Park Centres
Open daily April-October; limited in winter; closed in January

Aysgarth Falls	01969 662910	aysgarth@yorkshiredales.org.uk
Grassington	01756 751690	grassington@yorkshiredales.org.uk
Hawes	01969 666210	hawes@yorkshiredales.org.uk
Malham	01969 652380	malham@yorkshiredales.org.uk
Reeth	01748 884059	reeth@yorkshiredales.org.uk

Emergencies
If you have an accident whilst out walking and are immobilised, call 112 on your mobile 'phone, ask for the police, and tell them to contact mountain rescue. Be ready to tell the operator your exact location (nearest village, plus features named on the map close to your location) and the nature of your injury.

Weather
For the latest report for the Yorkshire Dales follow the link on the National Park website (see above) for 'Weather'. For details of local weather, go to **www. mylocalweather.org.uk** and click on the area you're interested in.